101 HILARIOUS DOG JOKES FOR KIDS

Laugh Out Loud With These Funny Jokes About Dogs (WITH 30+ PICTURES)!

© Copyright 2018 by Cesar Dunbar – All rights reserved.

In no way is it legal to reproduce, duplicate, or transmit any part of this document in either electronic means or in printed format. Recording of this publication is strictly prohibited and any storage of this document is not allowed unless with written permission from the publisher.

The information provided herein is stated to be truthful and consistent, in that any liability, in terms of inattention or otherwise, by any usage or abuse of any policies, processes, or directions contained within is the solitary and utter responsibility of the recipient reader. Under no circumstances will any legal responsibility or blame be held against the author for any reparation, damages, or monetary loss due to the information herein, either directly or indirectly.

The information herein is offered for informational purposes solely, and is universal as so. The presentation of the information is without contract or any type of guarantee assurance.

Medical Disclaimer: The jokes contained in this book are not intended as a substitute for consulting with your veterinary physician. All matters regarding your puppy's health require medical supervision.

Legal Disclaimer: all images used in this book are designed by Freepik.

Table of Contents

INTRODUCTION

First joke: *Why did the dog cross the road?*

Answer: *To get to the 'barking' lot!*

Thank you for picking up a copy of '*101 Hilarious Dog Jokes For Kids*'.

Let me get straight to the point: If you want to laugh about dogs, you don't need this book. **All you need is a dog!**

You know what I'm talking about: it's a lazy Sunday afternoon, you're chilling on the couch, looking at your pooch. And within 30 seconds he's *doing something* – or even just *looking at you in that special way* – and next thing you know you're **rolling on the floor with laughter**!

Did that ever happen to you?

Seriously, if you don't own a dog: if you want cheap entertainment, **get a dog**! It'll be the *best* investment you'll ever make.

But, who knows:

- maybe you feel bad about laughing at your dog all the time
- or perhaps you don't own a dog yet and are in dire need of some woof-tastic comedy
- Or you are simply looking to share some laughs *with* your pooch.

Well, you have come to the right place!

This book is jam-packed with:

- **100+ hilarious dog jokes**, and
- **30+ funny illustrations**

that will have you *grin*, *LOL*, and *roar with laughter*.

So, I hope you are ready: **let's have a laugh about man's best friend!**

101 HILARIOUS DOG JOKES

1.

Q: What do you call a dog magician?

A: A labracadabrador!

2.

Q: What do you call a dog with a surround system?

A: A sub-woofer.

3.

Knock, knock!
Who's there?
Ron.
Ron who?
Ron a little faster, will you? There's a Pitbull
after us!

4.

Q: What did the dog say when he sat on sandpaper?

A: Ruff!

5.

Q: What do you get when you cross a race dog with a bumble bee?

A: A Greyhound Buzz

6.

Q: What do you call a large dog that meditates?

A: Aware wolf.

7.

Q: What do you call a frozen dog?

A: A pupsicle.

8.

Q: What do you get when you cross a dog and a calculator?

A: A friend you can count on.

9.

Q: What do you call a cold dog?

A: A Chili Dog

10.

Q: How are a dog and a marine biologist alike?

A: One wags a tail and the other tags a whale.

11.

Q: What do you get if you cross a dog with a frog?

A: A dog that can lick you from the other side of the road!

12.

Q: Why did the poor dog chase his own tail?

A: He was trying to make both ends meet!

13.

Q: What kind of dog chases anything red?

A: A Bulldog.

14.

Q: What is a dog's favorite instrument?

A: A trombone.

15.

Q: Why don't blind people like to sky dive?

A: Because it scares the hell out of their guide dog.

16.

Q: What is a dog's favorite city?

A: New Yorkie!

17.

Q: What kind of dog likes taking a bath?

A: A shampoodle!

18.

Q: What happens when a dog chases a cat into a geyser?

A: It starts raining cats and dogs.

19.

Q: What do you call a dog with no legs?

A: It doesn't matter: he's not going to come anyway.

20.

Q: Why does the dog bring toilet paper to the party?

A: Because he is a party pooper.

21.

Q: What dog can jump higher than a tree?

A: Any dog can jump higher than a tree, trees can't jump.

22.

Q: What did the cat say to the dog?

A: Check meow-t!

23.

Q: What do you get if you cross a dog and a cheetah?

A: A dog that chases cars – and catches them!

24.

I went to the zoo today, there was only one animal.

It was a Shih Tzu...

25.

Q: What happens when it rains cats and dogs?

A: You can step in a poodle!

26.

John: I have a dog that doesn't have a nose.
Bill: And how does he smell?
John: Awful!

27.

One day, a man visited his friend. When he walked into the living room, he found his friend playing chess with his dog.

Astonished, he watched the game for a couple of minutes. "*I can't believe my eyes!*" he exclaimed. "*That is the smartest dog I have ever seen.*"

To which his friend replied: "*Mwoah, he's not that smart. I've beaten him three games out of five.*"

28.

Q: How did the little Scottish dog react when he met the Loch Ness Monster?

A: He was Terrier-fied!

29.

Q: What is it called when a cat wins a dog show?

A: A CAT-HAS-TROPHY!

30.

Q: What do you call a dog that licks an electrical socket?

A: Sparky.

31.

One Saturday morning, a wife says to her husband: *"Our dog is so smart. He brings in the daily newspapers every single morning!"*

Her husband replies: *"Yes, he's a great dog, but lots of dogs can do that."*

"Yes, but we've never subscribed to any," the wife responded.

32.

Did you hear about the dog who had puppies on the sidewalk?

She was ticketed for littering!

33.

One day, a police officer was sitting in his car with his K9 partner in the back seat. A little girl approached the car and asked the officer: *"Is that a dog in the back seat?"*

The officer replied: *"Yep, it sure is!"*

To which the girl responded: *"Wow, what did he do?"*

34.

Q: What do you get if you cross a Golden Retriever with a telephone?

A: A golden receiver.

35.

While mending fences out on the range, a very religious cowboy lost his favorite Bible. He was devastated!

Three weeks later, however, a dog walked up to him, carrying that same Bible in its mouth.

The cowboy was astonished, he couldn't believe it! He took the precious book out of the dog's mouth, thanked him, went on his knees and exclaimed: "*It's a miracle!*".

To which the dog replied: "*Not really. Your name is written inside the cover.*"

36.

A man takes his Bulldog to the vet, because he is cross-eyed.

The vet says: "*Let's have a look*" and picks up the Bulldog to examine his eyes. After looking at his eyes for a while, the vet says: "*I'm going to have to put him down.*"

"*Wait, what?*" the man replies, "*Just because he is cross-eyed?*"

Vet: "*No, because he is really heavy!*"

37.

Q: Where does a Rottweiler sit in the cinema?

A: Anywhere it wants to.

38.

Q: What's more amazing than a talking dog?

A: A spelling bee.

39.

Q: Why did the dog cross the road twice?

A: He was trying to fetch a boomerang.

40.

Q: What's a dog's favorite kind of pizza?

A: Pupperoni.

41.

Q: What do you call a dog who designs buildings?

A bark-itect.

42.

On a dark night, a burglar breaks into a house.

As he reaches to steal some valuables, he hears a voice say: *"Jesus is watching you."*

Alarmed by the voice, the burglar jumps up and hides behind the curtain. He peaks around the corner but doesn't see anybody.

So, he goes back to the valuables and continues putting them in his bag.

"Jesus is watching you," the voice says once more.

This time, the burglar looks harder and he sees a parrot.

"Who are you?" he asks.

The parrot replies, "*Elijah.*"

"*Wait, what? Who on earth would call a parrot Elijah?*" the burglar responds, relieved that he is only chatting with a parrot.

"*I don't know,*" says Elijah, "*I guess the same kind of people that would call a Rottweiler Jesus.*"

43.

Q: Why did the poor dog chase his tail?

A: He was trying to make ends meet.

44.

Q: How do you stop a dog from barking in your front yard?

A: Put it in your back yard.

45.

Q: What do you call a dog with a Rolex?

A: A watch dog.

46.

A dog walks into a job center. "*Wow, a talking dog,*" says the clerk. "*With your talent, I'm sure we can find you a gig in the circus.*" "*The circus?*" says the dog, disappointed: "*What does a circus want with a plumber?*"

47.

Two friends were walking their dogs on a Friday afternoon. One had a Pitbull and the other had a Chihuahua.

Then the guy with the Pitbull said: *"I'm thirsty, let's get a drink in that bar over there."* To which his friend replied: *"I don't think they will allow our dogs in there."* The one with the Pitbull responded: *"Just follow my lead, trust me."*

The guy with the Pitbull put on a pair of sunglasses and walked into the bar. The bouncer at the door said: *"I'm sorry man, but there are no pets allowed inside."* The man with the Pitbull replied: *"But this is my guide dog, I am helpless without him!"*. Bouncer: *"A Pitbull?"*. The man: *"Yeah, they're using Pitbulls now too, they're amazing!"*. Bouncer: *"Okay, come on in."*

The other man then also put on his sunglasses. He thought: a Chihuahua is even more unbelievable, but it's worth a try. So, the bouncer stopped him, and said: "*Sorry no pets allowed.*" To which the man replied: "*This is my guide dog, I am lost without him.*" Bouncer: "*Really, a Chihuahua?*". To which the man replied: "*Whhaaat? They gave me a fricking Chihuahua?!*"

48.

A dog went to the post office to send a telegram. He took out a blank form and wrote: *"Woof. Woof. Woof. Woof. Woof. Woof. Woof. Woof. Woof."*

When he was done, he gave it to the clerk. The clerk looked at the paper and said to the dog: *"There are only 9 words here. We have a special offer: You could send another 'Woof' for the same price."*

To which the dog replied: *"Sorry, but that wouldn't make any sense at all!"*

49.

Q: What do you call a dog with a fever?

A: A hot dog.

50.

Q: What happened when the dog went to the flea circus?

A: He stole the show!

51.

Q: What do you get if you cross a dog and a lion?

A: Well you won't be getting any mail, that's for sure.

52.

Knock, knock!
Who's there?
Doughnut.
Doughnut who?
Doughnut pull my dog's tail, or he'll bite you!

53.

Q: What do your dog and a cellphone have in common?

A: They both have collar I.D.

54.

Q: What sort of clothes does a pet dog wear?

A: A petticoat!

55.

Q: What kind of dog did Dracula have?

A: A bloodhound.

56.

Q: What do you get when you cross a herding dog and a daisy?

A: A Collie-flower!

57.

Q: Why was the dog such a good storyteller?

He knew how to paws for dramatic effect.

58.

Q: What do scientist dogs do with bones?

A: Barium!

59.

Q: Why do dogs make terrible dance partners?

A: They've got two left feet!

60.

Q: What happens when you name your dog after Kim Kardashian?

A: You give a dog a bad name.

61.

Q: What kind of dog eats with their ears?

A: They all do! Who removes their ears before dinner?

62.

Q: What do you get when you try to cross a Pitbull with a computer?

A: A lot of bites.

63.

Q: Why can't dogs work the TV remote when watching Netflix?

A: Because they always hit the Paws button!

64.

Q: What happens when you cross a rooster, a Cocker Spaniel and a Poodle?

A: A Cockerpoodledoo!

65.

Q: What do you get when you cross a Doberman with a Saint Bernard's?

A: A dog that bites you *and* then goes to fetch help.

66.

Q: Why do dogs run in circles?

A: Because it's hard to run in squares!

67.

Q: What do dogs eat for breakfast?

A: Pooched eggs.

68.

Q: Why don't dogs bark at their feet?

A: Because it's not polite to talk back to your Paw.

69.

Q: What did the waiter say to the dog when he brought out her food?

A: Bone appétit!

70.

Q: Why shouldn't you bring your farty dog to an Apple store?

A: Because they don't have Windows!

71.

Q: How do fleas travel from place to place?

A: By itch-hiking!

72.

Q: What's a dog's favorite sound?

A: The dinner bell.

73.

Q: What do you call a sleeping Rottweiler?

A: Anything you like, just very quietly.

74.

My dog's been having a bad day. When I came home, I asked him: *"How's life?"*

All he said was: *"RUFF..."*

75.

Two dogs are sitting on opposite sides of a river. One dog yells to the other: *"How do I get to the other side of the river?"* The other dog replies: *"You ARE on the other side!"*

76.

At a Royal Dinner Party, a Pug farts.

The King turns to him and says: "*How dare you fart in front of me!*"

The Pug replies: "*I'm terribly sorry, your Highness, I didn't realize it was your turn!*"

77.

Q: What's a dog's favorite dessert?

A: Pupcakes!

78.

Q: Why did the snowman name his dog "Frost"?

A: Because he bites!

79.

Q: What did the dog say to the tree?

A: Bark

80.

Q: What did the hungry Dalmatian say after his meal?

A: *"That hit the spots!"*

81.

Q: What do you do if a dog chews your dictionary?

A: Take the words right out of his mouth!

82.

Q: Why did the dog sleep under the car?

A: Because he wanted to wake up oily.

83.

Knock, knock!
Who's there?
Ken.
Ken who?
Ken you walk the dog for me?

84.

Q: Did you hear about the dog who invented the knock knock joke?

A: She won the no-bell prize!

85.

Q: Which breed of dog is the quietest?

A: A hush puppy!

86.

Q: Which dog breed is guaranteed to laugh at all of your jokes?

A: A Chi-ha-ha!

87.

Q: What is the fastest dog in the world?

A: A Labraghini.

88.

Q: What do you get if you cross a Beatle and an Australian dog?

A: Dingo Starr!

89.

Q: What happened to the dog that swallowed a firefly?

A: It barked with de-light!

90.

Q: Where do dogs go after their tails fall off?

A: The re-tail store.

91.

Q: What's a dog's ideal job?

A: Barkeology

92.

Q: What do you get if you cross a sheepdog with a jelly?

A: The collie wobbles!

93.

Q: What do you call a black Eskimo dog?

A: A dusky husky!

94.

Q: What did the dog say to the flea?

A: Stop bugging me!

95.

Q: In what month do dogs bark the least?

A: February, it's the shortest month!

96.

A three-legged dog walks into a bar.

He says: *"I'm looking for the man who shot my paw!"*

97.

Q: What do you call a dog that can use the toilet?

A: A 'poo-dle'.

98.

Q: Why do Dog Vampires believe everything you tell them?

A: Because they're suckers!

99.

Q: When is a mom flea happy?

A: When her whole family has gone to the dogs.

100.

Q: Why did the dog stay in the shade?

A: Because he did not want to turn into a hot dog.

101.

A dog sits in a bar, sipping a whiskey.

A customer walks up to him and says, "*Wow, it's not often that I see a dog drinking bourbon here!*"

To which the dog replies: "*Yeah, but that's hardly a surprise at these prices.*"

OTHER BOOKS BY THE AUTHOR

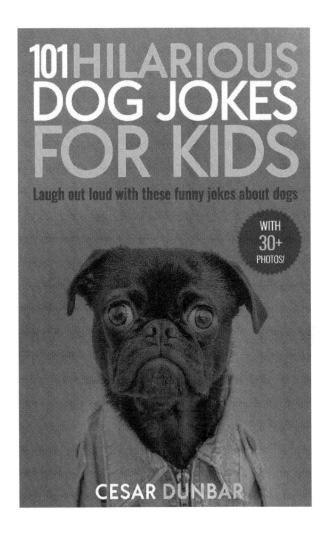

PUPPY
TRAINING 101
THE ESSENTIAL GUIDE TO
RAISING A PUPPY WITH LOVE

Train Your Puppy and Raise the Perfect Dog Through Potty Training,
Housebreaking, Crate Training and Dog Obedience

CESAR DUNBAR

DOG
TRAINING 101

THE ESSENTIAL GUIDE TO RAISING
A HAPPY DOG WITH LOVE

Train The Perfect Dog Through House Training,
Basic Commands, Crate Training and Dog Obedience.

CESAR DUNBAR

BONUS CHAPTER: HOW DOES A PUPPY THINK?

*This is a bonus chapter from my book '**Puppy Training 101**: The Essential Guide to Raising a Puppy With Love.' Enjoy!*

***

"There is no psychiatrist in the world like a puppy licking your face."

Bernard Williams

Ever wondered what your dog is thinking about? Read on to find out more. Would you like to know what your dog might be thinking? Wouldn't that be wonderful? Perhaps you have thought of a situation where your dog is able to clearly communicate with you. Unfortunately, this is nothing more than wishful thinking. However, you can develop a basic understanding of the psychology of your puppy.

***

Staring

"What are you thinking?" you might wonder, as your puppy is looking at you longingly. If you have already fed him and have also taken him out for a walk, it might be really difficult to figure out what he is thinking. Dogs tend to gaze at their owners, intently. Probably this isn't a sign of boredom. He is probably staring at you intently because he wants a treat, wants to play, or just wants you to pet him for a while. Your dog might also be doing this because he wants some extra attention and love.

***

Looking Sad

Do you feel really guilty when you leave your puppy home alone and head out to work the whole day? You might worry that your dog would be sad the whole day. Unless your puppy has separation anxiety, your puppy will be perfectly fine. In fact, if you have a dog walker checking in on your dog, then the puppy would greet him with a wagging tail. Your puppy might seem confused or even sad when you leave, but they tend to get used to your routine. They tend to adapt themselves to it. However, it is really important that your dog knows the difference between your usual work schedule and a long trip.

***

Barking Repeatedly

Does your puppy tend to keep barking whole night long? It might seem like the only reason he's doing this is to keep you from getting any sleep. You will need to remember that they bark for a particular reason. Your puppy isn't barking to annoy you. Your puppy might be doing this to get your attention. A dog usually barks when it wants something. Perhaps a treat, to go on a walk, or even to be freed from its confinement. It could also be because your puppy senses danger and he wants to let you know. Or he is excited and wants to play with you. Dogs tend to learn by repeating their behaviors. If your puppy has discovered that by barking, he gets something that he wants, he will keep on doing it.

***

Cocking Their Head

You might have noticed that your dog tends to tilt his head to the side when you speak to him. This is definitely not because your puppy understands the story you are telling him. They tend to cock their head for multiple reasons. Your puppy might be hoping to better understand a word you are saying, or something that sounds familiar. Your puppy might also be cocking his head so that he can hear you better. Or perhaps to get a better look at your face to understand what you are saying.

Attempting to understand what goes on within your puppy's mind is an ongoing practice. After a while, you will be able to understand what your dog wants by just one look of theirs.

***

This is the end of this bonus chapter.

Want to continue reading?

Then go to the Amazon website and search for "puppy training 101"

THE ESSENTIAL GUIDE TO
RAISING A PUPPY WITH LOVE

Train Your Puppy and Raise the Perfect Dog Through Potty Training,
Housebreaking, Crate Training and Dog Obedience

CESAR DUNBAR

Hope to see you there!

19091461R10071

Made in the USA
Middletown, DE
04 December 2018